THE
WILDERNESS
EXPERIENCE

LIFE IN THE SADDLE

WRITINGS AND PHOTOGRAPHS

SELECTED AND EDITED BY

GRETEL EHRLICH

A Harvest Original

HARCOURT BRACE & COMPANY

SAN DIEGO • NEW YORK • LONDON

A TEHABI BOOK

Requests for permission to make copies of any part of the work should be mailed to: Permissions Department, Harcourt Brace & Company, 6277 Sea Harbor Drive, Orlando, Florida 32887-6777.

Ivan Doig, excerpt from *This House of Sky: Landscapes of a Western Mind* by Ivan Doig. Copyright © 1978 by Ivan Doig, reprinted by permission of Harcourt Brace & Company and the author.

Frank Harris, excerpt from *My Reminiscences as a Cowboy* by Frank Harris (1855–1931). Copyright © 1930. Published by Charles Boni, Jr., 1930, New York.

Dayton O. Hyde, excerpt from *Wilderness Ranch* by Dayton O. Hyde. Copyright © 1971 by Dayton O. Hyde. *Wilderness Ranch* was originally published by The Dial Press under the title *Yammi*. Reprinted by permission of Dayton O. Hyde and John Hawkins, Inc.

William Kittredge, "The Promised Generation," excerpt from *Hole in the Sky* by William Kittredge. Copyright © 1992 by William Kittredge. Reprinted by permission of Alfred A. Knopf, Inc.

Thomas McGuane, "Roping from A to B," excerpt from *An Outside Chance: Essays on Sport* by Thomas McGuane. Copyright © 1969, 1970, 1971, 1972, 1973, 1974, 1976, 1977, 1978, 1979, 1980 by Thomas McGuane. Reprinted by permission of author's agent International Creative Management, Inc., New York.

Thomas McGuane, "Another Horse," excerpt from *An Outside Chance: Essays on Sport* by Thomas McGuane. Copyright © 1969, 1970, 1971, 1972, 1973, 1974, 1976, 1977, 1978, 1979, 1980 by Thomas McGuane. Reprinted by permission of International Creative Management, Inc., New York.

Mark Spragg, "In Praise of Horses" by Mark Spragg. First appeared in *Northern Lights* magazine Vol IX, No. 1. Used with permission of Mark Spragg.

Library of Congress Cataloging-in-Publication Data
Life in the Saddle: writings and photographs/selected and edited by Gretel Ehrlich; photographs by award-winning photographers.
 p.   cm.— (The Wilderness experience)
"A Tehabi book."
ISBN 0-15-600226-4 (pbk.)
 1. Horses—West (U.S.)—Anecdotes.   2. Ranchers—West (U.S.)—Anecdotes.   3. Horsemanship—West (U.S.)—Anecdotes.
4. Horses—West (U.S.)—Pictorial works.   5. Ranchers—West (U.S.)—Pictorial works.   6. Horsemanship—West (U.S.)—Pictorial works.
I. Ehrlich, Gretel.   II. Series.
SF301.L72 1995
798.2´3´0978—dc20   95-12541

Life in the Saddle was produced by Tehabi Books. Nancy Cash–*Series Editor and Developmental Editor*; Laura Georgakakos–*Manuscript Editor*; Sam Lewis–*Project Art Director*; Andy Lewis–*Art Director;* Tom Lewis–*Editorial and Design Director*; Sharon Lewis–*Controller*; Chris Capen–*President*.

Harcourt Brace & Company and Tehabi Books, in association with The Basic Foundation, a not-for-profit organization whose primary mission is reforestation, will facilitate the planting of two trees for every one tree used in the manufacture of this book. This edition is printed on acid-free paper that meets the American National Standards Institute Z39.48 Standard.

Printed in Hong Kong through Mandarin Offset.
First edition 1995
A B C D E

CONTENTS

LIFE IN THE SADDLE

Life in the saddle—life with horses—began in the American West in 1547 when the Spanish explorer, Pedro de Casteneda, reintroduced horses to the Plains. The horse had been indigenous to the Americas but had become extinct. Now these "mystery dogs," as some Native Americans described them, were brought back as beasts of burden with all the accoutrements of the Spanish horseman, which we've appropriated as our own—the saddle, bridle, chaps, and spurs—though, in fact, it was not the Europeans who developed the stirrup and saddle, but the Chinese.

The adoption of the horse by the North American Plains Indians changed the lives of indigenous people here. The range of the hunter vastly increased, herds of bison moved farther and faster, tribes that had been sedentary became nomadic, and the horse was pressed into use as a way to make intertribal raids and wars.

The warhorse became the farm and ranch horse, a steed used to plow fields and work sheep and cattle, and horse breeding and horsemanship became a badge of pride and honor in the American West, beginning with the Spaniards and Californios, then the Native Americans, and finally the white explorers and settlers who visited and populated the grass-filled basins and towering ranges of the West.

Stories about horses have abounded since those times. Books for children and adults, from *The Virginian* to *Black Beauty,* have been a hallmark of American life. The flared nostrils, pricked ears, and flowing tail of a horse—all that raw, wind-loving beauty—belies an acutely sensitive nature. Keen-eyed, horses pick up on subtleties of gesture and mood and can see into us by the look in our eyes and by the way we move.

The balancing act between humans and horses has been at the center of western life and remains there today. We need the horse to do our ranchwork, and the horse, willing to be used and wanting to please, has the power to bite, kick, sideswipe, and buck us off almost effortlessly.

We make deals with our horses: sometimes we simply try to sneak in a ride while "breaking" a colt while other times we attempt to develop trust and harmony with the animal, not only out of respect for him, but out of self-preservation. Fatal horsewrecks are not uncommon and at the least, a fall can hurt one's pride.

Life in the Saddle is a collection of contemporary accounts by those of us who were raised with horses and, for at least some part of our lives, have accomplished our daily tasks on their backs. The book didn't start out this way. I pored over the canon of western Americana, through stirring accounts of the finding and founding of the West in the saddle, including ranching and hunting stories by Theodore Roosevelt, an exploration of the Rockies by Isabelle Bird, an account of homesteading by Eleanor Pruitt Stewart, a journal of wandering by Joseph Le Conte, cowboying in Texas by Charlie Siringo, a ride through California by Edwin Bryant, and many, many more.

But somewhere along the way, I developed a fondness for these eight accounts by men and women of and in the West. They offer fresh insights into the difficulties and joys of working with animals. No cowboy glamour here, but the real thing: lots of buckoffs, aching muscles, practical jokes, humor, and general dismay in a world whose harshness and grandeur is almost unspeakable.

I came to love Tom McGuane's humor, Mark Spragg's lyricism, Bill Kittredge's blunt honesty, Dayton Hyde's sure-footedness, Ivan Doig's chumminess, and the poignancy of Laura Bell's account of sheepherding on the Wyoming range.

Unlike Bill, Ivan, and Dayton, I wasn't ranch-raised but rode horses in utero and later, sleepwalked to our stable to sleep with them, preferring straw to a bed. It was only in my late twenties that I began living and working on ranches, finally owning one, which is never as much fun as "riding the grubline." But once you've gained that kind of intimacy with a place, it never leaves you. You are marked by that landscape and the horses you rode.

Each writer here has known the glories and defeats of life in the saddle. Each has nursed broken bones, been lost, been tricked and saved by the horses each has ridden, and has tried to map the horses' minds as they do ours.

The best thing about being on horseback is the view it affords. Riding high off the ground we can see a hundred miles to snowy mountains ahead, or the anvil-shaped thundercloud rising into a summer sky. In a hard winter, I once dropped down between two draft horses hitched to the haywagon to get warm; at a lonely sheepcamp, a horse has been my only company; and when the clouds have socked in on a high benchland—all visibility gone—my horse brought me home. May this small offering of horse stories keep you warm, keep you company, teach you to see, and carry you home. *—Gretel Ehrlich*

A SENSE OF HORSE

Mark Spragg was born and raised with horses on the North Fork of the Shoshone River, which flows down from Yellowstone Park's high plateau toward the town of Cody, Wyoming. This evocative essay on his boyhood is a lyric of growing up with horses and the ways in which they taught him to see. Though widely traveled, Mark lives in northwestern Wyoming and writes essays and screenplays. He has recently completed a novel. —G. E.

From *In Praise of Horses* by

MARK SPRAGG

When I was a boy my father had horses, over a hundred of them, some of them rank, and I sat them well. He believed that horses were to use and that boys were nothing if not used and that by putting me with horses he was tending to some grand plan of economy.

When we did not have them in the mountains, packed with foodstuffs, duffels, or dudes, we worked them at the ranch. In the kidney-warm manure cake of the corrals, in the ridden to dust round corral. They milled, roiling like a vast pod of smallish whales, multi-colored, snorting at their handicapped buoyancy, rolling their eyes white at me, a boy who had come to straddle their hearts.

I walked among them clumsily, not much used to walking, having spent so many hours attached to them. They moved away from me, parting, and in my wake would re-adhere into a whole of watchfulness. It was my job to remind them of the union of man and horse, to ride them, to ride the younger ones again and again until they became convinced that I was part of them and other men a part of me.

In the evenings I turned them out of the corrals and hazed them upstream in a tight valley and left them to fan and separate and feed. They grazed the rifts and slant of the young mountain range, their shod hooves striking sparks from the granite in the night, their senses sparked keenly to the dangers of the night.

In the mornings, before four in the morning, I gathered them, riding in the dark, hearing the bells put around the necks of the leaders of the different clans of this tribe of horses separate like the parts of a simple chord, spread wide, sounding in resonance their prehistoric energies. I brought them together thundering through downfall, scree, and fast water, impossibly up and down the steep and careless landscape, back to the corrals, where I would spend the day reviving their marriage to me.

I was a boy, and I believed deeply in the sightedness of horses. I believed that there was nothing that they did not witness. I believed that to have a horse between my legs, to extend my pulse and blood and energy to theirs enhanced my vision. Made of me a seer. I believed them to be the dappled, sorrel, roan, bay, black pupils in the eyes of God.

I worried over my love of them, I wondered at our connectedness. I looked for hazard through their eyes. I scented the earth and the wind that swirled across the earth with their wide nostrils. I felt the gravity in river water against my legs and stomach, my hooves skating for balance on the round and moss-covered rocks of streambeds. I nibbled at the world with their blunt, soft lips. I felt them drowsy between my legs, enraged, frightened, straining in their solid work. I felt the rare ones reach exhaustion and reach past it to drain a last reservoir of spirit, dammed with horse pride, and when it was drained I felt them reach again and use its muddy bottom to fuel themselves, and once sat a horse that trembled and staggered and had no more to give. An animal who had come to the bedrock of himself. He fell, and I fell with him. I held his head on my knees and laid the side of my face against his flat forehead and wept and whispered to him that my life was draining into his and that I knew it was not enough. And yet, I emptied myself into him. I prayed aloud for the strength to lift and carry him to safety. The night blurred our peripheries and brought us close to death, and still I chanted my whispered prayers for union. In early light we got to our feet and cautiously through the trees to home, where I vowed never to extend my stamina past my adolescent strength.

On days out of the mountains, at midday, with the sun hotly at me, I would slump in the shade close to the noise and smell of them and reconstruct a fantasy that made me happy. In this midday dream I was on a horse, on the back of a mixed blood, a mutt gently broken to saddle, unshod, a feral and unfettered thing; a horse with the heart of a flowering herb, windblown and glad to bloom at the peripheries of husbandry. I was a boy who rode wildly in his dreams. Startled when I woke from them that my body was so little haired, held upright by two thin legs.

In the afternoon I rode the colts. The young ones who could be counted on to rupture into the air and to earth again, and again, twisting, grunting, screaming in their rage, bent on divorce from me. And when exhausted, finding me still part of them, would stand quivering, sweating their hot, sweet scent to further foment my intoxication with them. I took no pride in riding them down. It was simply the use we made of one another, and I felt smaller for their loss of recklessness.

A dozen times each summer, in the hot late part of the summer, I would ride a dark, sun-sleeked horse to a meadow above the ranch. A long, tight valley bordered by timber and bare rock mountain, the home of a smooth stream lost from view in the waist-deep grass and late wildflowers. Beside this stream I would strip us of clothes, saddle, boots, bridle and remount cleanly, my naked heels against naked ribs, my buttocks clenched on the warm, haired spine, and ride stiffly into the water.

On the short, straight stretches the animal walked warily, as though on the skulls of mice, belly-deep in the water, its hooves sucking at the graveled bottom. And in the bends, the water squeezed into a thick emerald green against green banks overhung with green grass we would have to swim. I would grip the tuft of hair at the nape of its mane and rise toward the sun, slowly towed as the animal momentarily fell away from me, cooling in the water, lightly connected by our heat only. Connected more vastly by a sense of movement past the heat that we could make.

At night my dreams had more grandeur than those I could muster in the sun. At night I lived on the back of a horse and fasted. I lay along its back, my mouth open in the rain, collecting water and ozone. I slept draped forward on its neck, my arms hanging to the sides of its neck in loose embrace, my hands clenching in my sleep to grasp and hold the vision that grazed beneath me. I breathed into the coarse, dark mane, my lungs filled with the salted taste of horses.

In my sleep before dawn I would stand on its rump and urinate and afterward scream my naked, gaunt presence into the vault of the black, night sky, unsilhouetted; leaked into the lightless ether.

And in my dream I would ride this horse, oddly, often a pinto, dark-eyed, dark-nostriled, dark-stockinged with one white hoof, front left, slightly softer than the darker three, striking the earth in a tone a third lower, making music as it ran.

And I would know, sitting upright on this horse, my arms held high and wide, that when a horse is hot and lathered and running toward the curve of the earth all four feet, regardless of color, leave the ground at once and that in those suspended moments relaxed from effort the rider and ridden are afforded, for that instant, and the next and the next after that, the sight of God.

I am a boy no longer. I am a man now who works away from horses, who lives in a common blindness, seeing with his eyes only. But a man with a remembered glimpse of sightedness. And it is horses that I have to thank. ❧

MY DAD'S LIFE

Ivan Doig gives us a portrait of his father, Charlie Doig, who herded sheep and cow-boyed in central Montana in the early 1900s. To Charlie, who relished every confrontation, the horse was a bucking machine. Ivan's 1978 book, This House of Sky, *is a memoir of Charlie's early colorful years. Ivan eventually migrated from the open spaces of Montana to Seattle where he lives with his wife, Carol. He has authored several books including a number of historical novels. —G. E.*

Excerpts from *This House of Sky* by

IVAN DOIG

But the deep ingredient of my father's adventuring in those years of his early twenties was horses. It was a time when a man still did much of his day's work atop a saddle pony, and the liveliest of his recreation as well. And with every hour in the saddle, the odds built that there was hoofed catastrophe ahead. Built, as Dad's stories lessoned into me, until the most casual swing into the stirrups could almost cost your life: *I'll tell ye a time. I was breakin' this horse, and I'd rode the thing for a couple of weeks, got him pretty gentle—a big nice tall brown horse with a stripe in his face. I'd been huntin' elk up in the Castles, and I'd rode that horse all day long. Comin' home, I was just there in the Basin below the Christison place, and got off to open a gate. My rifle was on the saddle there, with the butt back toward the horse's hip, and it'd rubbed a sore there and I didn't notice the rubbin'. When I went to get back on, took hold of the saddle horn to pull myself up, ye know, the rifle scraped across that sore. Boy, he ducked out from under me and I went clear over him. I caught my opposite foot in the stirrup as I went over, and away he went, draggin' me. He just kicked the daylights out of me as we went. It was in a plowed field, and I managed to turn over and get my face like this—*cradling his arms in front of his face, to my rapt watching—*but he kept kickin' me in*

17

the back of the head here, until he had knots comin' on me big as your fist. And he broke my collarbone. Finally my boot came off, or he'd of dragged me around until he kicked my head off, I guess.

The accident of flailing along the earth with a horse's rear hooves thunking your skull was one thing. Courting such breakage was another, and it was in my father not to miss that chance, either. Most summer Sundays, the best riders in the county would gather at a ranch and try to ride every bucking horse they had been able to round up out of the hills. It was the kind of hellbending contest young Charlie Doig was good at, and he passed up few opportunities to show it.

The hill broncs which would be hazed in somewhere for this weekend rodeoing—the Doig homestead had a big stout notched-pole corral which was just right—were not scruffy little mustangs. They were half again bigger and a lot less rideable than that: herds grown from ranch stock turned out to pasture, with all the heft of workhorses added to their new wildness. Eventually there came to be a couple of thousand such renegades roaming the grassed hills around the valley. Some would weigh more than three-quarters of a ton and measure almost as tall at the shoulder as the height of a big man. A rider would come away from a summer of those massive hill broncs with one experience or another shaken into his bones and brain, and Dad's turn came up when the last two horses were whooped into the Doig corral at dusk one of those Sunday afternoons.

Five or six of us were ridin', all had our girls there and were showin' off, ye know. Neither of the last horses looked worth the trouble of climbing on—a huge club-hoofed bay, and a homely low-slung black gelding. Someone yelled out, *That black one looks like a damned milk cow!* Dad called across the corral to the other rider, *Which one of those do you want, Frankie, the big one or that black thing?* The bay was saddled, and thudded around the corral harmlessly on its club hooves. Then the corral crew roped the black for Dad and began to discover that this one was several times more horse than it looked. *Oh, he was a bearcat, I'm here to tell you.*

The gelding was so feisty they had to flop him flat and hold him down to cinch the saddle on, the last resort for a saddling crew that took any pride in itself. Dad swung into the stirrups while the horse was uncoiling up out of the dirt. When the bronc had all four feet under him, he sunfished for the corral poles and went high into them as intentionally as if he were a suicide plunging off a cliff. Horse and rider crashed back off the timers, then the bronc staggered away into another quick running start and slammed the fence again. And then again.

He like to have beat my brains out on that corral fence. Then, worse: *He threw me off over his head upside down and slammed me against that log fence again, and still he kept a-buckin'. I jumped up and got out of his way and tried to climb the fence.* Dad had made it onto the top of the fence when the battering caught up with his body. Blacking out, he pitched off the corral backwards, into the path of the gelding as it rampaged past. The horse ran over him full length, full speed. *One hoof hit me in the ribs here, and the other hit me in the side of the head here, and just shoved all the skin down off the side of my face in a bunch.* The gelding would have hollowed him out like a trough if the corral crew hadn't managed to snake Dad out under the fence before the horse could get himself turned. By then, someone already was sprinting for a car for the forty-five–mile ride to a doctor. *I was laid up six weeks that time, before I could even get on crutches.*

That was his third stalking by death; Dad himself had invited most of the risk that time, although in the homely black gelding it came by the sneakiest of means. But the next near-killing hit him as randomly as a lightning bolt exploding a snag. It began with the yip of coyote pups on a mountainside above the Basin. *I was workin' for Bert Plymale, and we lambed a bunch of sheep over there near the D.L. place.* Coyotes, sheep killers that they were, were hated as nothing else in that country, especially on the lean foothill ranches where any loss of livestock hurt like a wound. *They were eatin' the lambs just about as fast as we could turn 'em out. And we could hear these coyotes in a park up on the side of the mountain, yippin' up there early morning and evening. So I had a young kid workin' with me, and we decided we'd go up there and find that den.*

When they reined up in a clearing in the timber where the yips were coming from, Dad stepped off his horse and walked ahead a few steps to look for the den. *I was carryin' the pick and the kid was carryin' the shovel—in case we found the den, we could dig it out. I'd stepped off of this bay horse, dropped the lines and walked several feet in front of him, clear away from him. That sap of a kid, he dropped that shovel right at the horse's heels. And instead of kickin' at the shovel like a normal horse would, ye know, he jumped ahead and whirled and kicked me right in the middle of the back. Drove two ribs into my lungs.*

Dad hunched on the ground like a shot animal. *I couldn't get my breath atall when I'd try to straighten up. When I was down on all fours, I could get enough breath to get by on. The kid, he was gonna leave me there and take off to find everybody in the country to come get me with a stretcher. I said no, by God, I was gonna get out of there somehow.* Spraddled on hands and knees in a red fog of pain, he gasped out to the youngster to lead his horse beneath a small cliff nearby. Dad crawled to the cliff, climbed off the ledge into the saddle. Then, crumpled like a dead man tied into the stirrups, he rode the endless mile and a half to the ranch. *That was one long ride, I'm-here-to-tell-you.*

Getting there only began a new spell of pain—the pounding car ride across rutted roads to town and the doctor. By then, Dad's breathing had gone so ragged and bloody that the doctor set off with him for the hospital in Bozeman. Two gasping hours more in a car. At last, by evening, he lay flat in a hospital bed. *But I always healed fast, anyway,* and a few weeks later, he climbed stiffly onto a horse again.

He wouldn't have thought, when he was being battered around from one near-death to the next, that he was heading all the while into the ranch job he would do for many of the rest of his years. But the valley, which could always be counted on to be fickle, now was going to let him find out in a hurry what he could do best. Sometime in 1925, when he was twenty-four years old, Dad said his goodbyes at the Basin homestead another time, saddled up, and rode to the far end of the Smith River Valley to ask for a job at the Dogie ranch. ❧

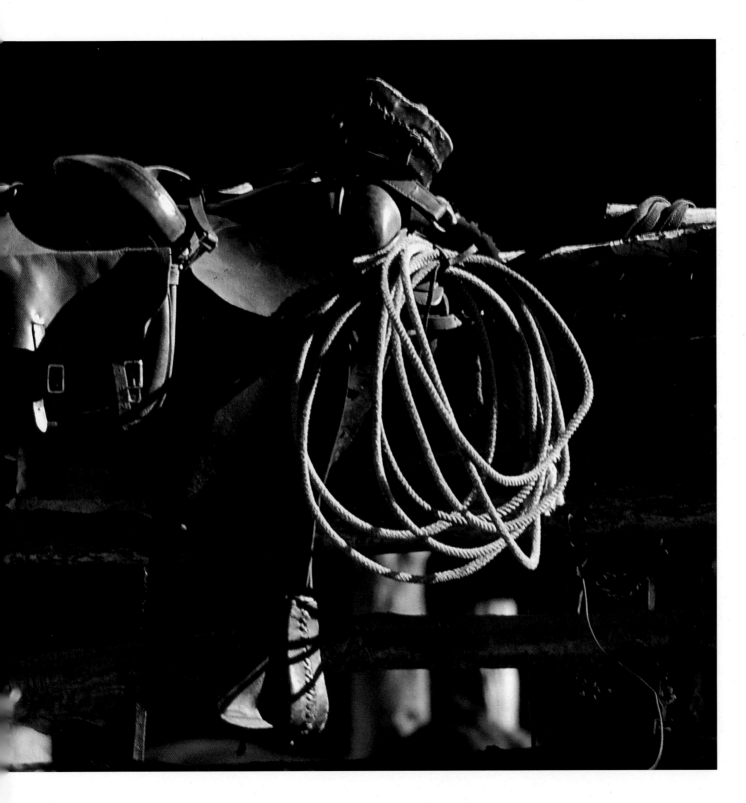

RIDING THE GRUBLINE

Horses have been a part of my life from the beginning—as companions, as coworkers, as friends. During the years I've lived among them and during the years I've lived far away, they've remained a part of me through all that they teach and through the views that their backs afford. —G. E.

Sleepwalking to Horses by

GRETEL EHRLICH

I used to walk in my sleep—from bed to window, from window to barn, and once there, into a straw-bedded stall surrounded by the sound and smell of horses.

Our house sat in the middle of horse pastures filled with broodmares, colts, fillies, as well as the saddle horses we rode. One could say I began riding before I was born, since my mother was frequently on horseback with me in utero.

By the age of seven, I had my own string: an old mare called Rosebud, a palomino that was part Chincoteague pony named Sprint, a pony named Blackie, and a mare named Lisa. Each afternoon I rode them one by one, often wandering alone into the mountains atop what I peevishly told my parents was "my only friend."

The view from horseback was my vantage point. Small for my age, moving about the world aboard such a large animal was akin to having wings. While other children were transported by parents, I rode to the local soda fountain, the beach, the hobo camp, and, on the 4th of July, all the way into town to join the parade.

Roans, bays, sorrels, chestnuts, and palominos populated my dreams, walking on oceans and galloping on air; and in my waking life they were sure, kind, and peaceful—qualities I was having trouble finding in human beings.

Twenty-three years later, after an urban existence in New York and Los Angeles, horseflesh once again dominated my thoughts and their powerful, graceful bodies carried me through each day. For fifteen years I "rode the grubline" in northern Wyoming, moving from ranch to ranch with my saddle horses and cowboying for three or four different ranchers.

June. Stan sent me out to gather the last of the cows and calves from the home place and trail them to spring range. Western meadowlarks nested in dry stalks flew up as the horse and I approached. My young horse jumped. Ahead were the cattle. I looked for a river crossing. High water broke brown and white against mid-stream boulders. Steam rose from a quiet eddy and it was there that I crossed. My horse had never been in water this fast and deep, and he put his nose to it and blew hard. The current drove against his legs making him waver. On the other side he jumped, lost his footing, stumbled and tried to buck. I thought I better give the horse something to do quickly before he bucked me off.

I rode behind the cattle at a trot, whooping at them to move out. Finally they started into the water, now stained pink by dawn. By 9 A.M., we reach the Beef slide, a wide, straight-up trail to the top of the mountain. The cattle hang back, slow down, lazy in hot morning sun. Bathed in sun, bathed in dust, I put my neck scarf over my nose and mouth. The calves run back and we turn to get them, bringing a few cows along to lead the way back up the mountain.

We "noon up" at the first waterhole, eating sandwiches made at 3 A.M., long before ham and cheese looked appetizing. I unsaddle my young horse and let him graze while enjoying sun and the cool breeze on his back. He's a light-mouthed, leggy two-year-old from cutting horse stock, and has a clownish temperament. Instead of grazing, he stands over me then picks up my sack lunch in his mouth and swings it around over my head. When I offer him cheese, he curls up his lip and saunters away.

Afternoon. A storm breaks over us just as we try to move the cattle over a bridge. Thunder blasts and the echoing of hooves on the bridge send the cattle running back through us as if we four riders were a sieve. Gathered up again, we push them across, now in drenching rain, and into a holding pasture for the night.

Riding a young horse through a season of work results in an intimate understanding of one another. When I get on in the morning, he knows a lot more about my state of mind than I do. And I try to know a little about his. If I'm unsure, he's unsure; if I'm upset, he behaves unpredictably; if I can keep the trust that has spawned between us, we move through the day smoothly with a deep physical harmony like no other.

July. Dawn again. Today we are moving cattle from the pasture called Hazel Early to Granite Pass. One bull hides in a thicket of pine trees, obsessed, not only with shading his muscled body from sun, but, apparently, from moonlight as well. Rode point all day, which means I rode just behind the head of the herd and attempted to guide them—more often they were guiding me—down a trail, across a creek, through timber, emerging onto a patch of snow.

When moving a large herd of animals, riders are assigned to ride point, flank, or drag point being the trickiest. If you ride too far ahead, the whole herd will turn back; if you get too far behind the lead cow, she'll take off and go the wrong way. Riding point hones the skill of maintaining balance. It's a lesson in anticipating accurately what's coming up and a reminder that too much speed and aggression loses the day.

On a wide flat we stop to doctor a calf for pinkeye. We get our ropes down, flailing through sagebrush after the animal. My loop gets caught on the first bush, I slow down to make another loop, but Mart, another rider, already has the calf caught. As he takes his dallies—secures his lariat to his saddle horn—the horse bucks, gets tangled in the rope and falls down. Mart emerges grinning. Another two cowboys take over, heading and heeling the calf and I stand by to squeeze powder into the afflicted eye.

Just as we reach Granite Pass and the gate after which there is nothing but high, craggy alpine country, another thunderstorm breaks its black neck over the herd as they run downhill to water. We ride back down the highway as fast as we can to waiting horsetrailers.

August. The sting has gone out of the sun, and thunderstorms soften into all-day rains. Weeks before, I was armoring myself from sun with a hat, dark glasses, and white shirt. Now I'm in longjohns, bundled in jackets and gloves wishing for sun to mend my aching bones.

Yesterday I had an accident. Stupidly tied a horse to a rail instead of a post, and when he pulled back the whole rail came with him, tied to the reins. As I tried to get out of the way, the rail banged me on the head, the back, and across the backs of my legs, knocking me over. Later, riding to the cattle, a rattlesnake struck at my horse's front foot. . . . August swayed into September.

A horse is such a timorous being. His mind is pure and innocent and he wants to please. Each year I rode a young horse with Ray Hun, a trainer who broke us from saying we were "breaking a horse," who taught us to teach a colt not through control and force, but trust and release, so that the life could move freely through the body. The image of the cowboy bucking out a colt in a round corral has done much to damage the equine-human interaction. It intimates domination, fear, and injury. Now, during each long summer of work, I try to do less and less with a colt, giving him less resistance, letting him stay united within himself, and together, finding a way to get where we are going.

The walking speed of the horse is a bit faster than that of the human, and the elevated ride is quiet, smooth, and peaceful. There is a regality to a horse's fine back and powered hips, his arching neck and flicking ears—those sensitive, fine-tuned antennas. My head lines up with the horse's. The space between his ears are the sights through which I see the world.

To work and move around on the back of another sentient being—the horse—is an intimate proposition. He mirrors me and I mirror him; we are conjoined and come alive as one being. Nothing is hidden between us: his fear or mine, the strength and fatigue, skittishness and grace that ebb and flow from each to the other throughout the day.

Fall roundup in the Wolf Mountains of Montana is a month-long job. This is an old-fashioned ranch with a chuck wagon and no holding pastures. If you have to ride a fifty-mile circle to and from the cattle each day, then that's your job.

We started in the dark. Breakfast was at 3:30. Six horses were roped out of the remuda and saddled. We rode out, six abreast at a hard trot and didn't stop trotting for three hours. A cold wind blew off the ridges. Because the moon was new, it was hard to see.

One morning a young coyote followed us, loping along behind my horse. If I stopped to look at him, he crouched, but as soon as I began trotting, he followed along. Every morning was the same—riding fast in a hard silence, too cold and bone-tired to talk. Three riders loped ahead climbing a high knot, and two others disappeared down a separate drainage. I was told to wait. Soon enough, just at first light, cattle began pouring off the hills toward me. My job was to gather them and keep them moving. Hundreds of animals came down to me and I loped my horse up to the lead, turning the herd, then back to the drag to pick up strays. Back and forth I raced, wondering if I was turning them in the proper direction, wondering why I had been left alone.

We gathered 1,500 head that day. By 9 A.M. I changed to a fresh horse. The other riders reappeared and we strung out cattle as far as the eye could see. At the sorting corrals, 25 miles from where we had started with the cattle, five semis and three brand inspectors awaited us. Changed horses again. We paraded the cattle by the inspectors so they could read the brands to make sure we weren't in the business of stealing livestock. Then we sorted for weight and pushed the animals down a wide alleyway into the trucks. The sound of yelling and hooves on metal was cacophony.

Each day was the same. The silences in the mornings lasted longer as our tiredness grew, but the stories at the end of the day after dinner, expanded. One night, Mike, my cowboying partner and I went to Hardin with one of the men. We drank at the Three Aces Bar, danced for awhile, and then drove to Charlie's ranch to get fresh horses. As we loaded six geldings, I looked north. The sky had swollen into a bruise, then a palette of pulsing light. Far to the west a line of black storm clouds approached, the northern lights shooting through them as if to dispel the rain. The horses stomped restlessly in the trailer. They could smell the storm, and as rain began to fall, turning quickly to snow, the aurora was the last ray of light holding back the desolation of winter. ❧

OF LARIATS AND HORSEFLESH

Thomas McGuane confesses that growing up in the Midwest, he despised horses. But something changed along the way. Today he's a rancher who ropes and cuts with the best of them. And having made that 180-degree change, he's all humor about himself and awed by the horse. Almost no one writes as well about horseflesh as McGuane does.
—G. E.

Excerpts from *An Outside Chance* by

THOMAS MCGUANE

I grew up in the Midwest and despised horses. The ones I rode struck me as stupid and untrustworthy. I went to Wyoming when I was young, and the ones there were worse. On a cold morning, two out of three would buck you down. They were, I felt, an ugly necessity for where a truck wouldn't go.

I've been kicked, stepped on, and bitten. Bitten I liked least. My most trustworthy saddle horse leaned over once while I was cinching him up and clamped on my upper leg, turning the thigh into what looked a Central American sunset. I threw him down on the ground, half hitched his feet together, and put a tarp over him. I let him up two hours later; he thought I was the greatest man in the world, one he wouldn't think of biting. Horses only remember the end of the story. . . .

Then, a decade ago, I made some money and bought a ranch in Montana. That's where I am now, writing this loopy roping story.

I bought a saddle horse named Cayenne who is supposed to go back to Yellow Jacket; and for the first time I began to ride in the normal course of things—knocking around, going in the hills, checking ditches and head gates. I still have this horse. He's a big easy-keeping sorrel with a blaze on his face; above all, a sensible horse.

He really taught me the coming and going aspects of a using horse: how their feet move in the rocks, when they're winded, how much water they need when they're hot, how you shouldn't let them eat when you're gathering cattle or they learn to dive at a gallop because idle hunger has struck; why you should get down when your lariat is caught under your horse's tail, why nose flies make them throw their heads in your face, why geldings make that noise at a trot, why Old Paint will always walk off and leave you; how a horse will, finally, sell out for grain, how a horse can get you home from the mountains in the dark when a mule can't; and above all how, when you do such things long enough with one horse, you begin to see things in him, to look deep in his eyes and to make your deal, which is a kind of interchange of respect.

Once when I was trimming Cayenne's feet, I thought he was leaning his weight on me and I thumped him with the rasp. He wouldn't eat for the rest of the day. The rasp certainly didn't hurt him. Now that I think of it, I offered him oats and he never sold out. There was a specific deal between that horse and me; and I had violated it. I never did it again. There was no question that I had hurt his feelings. At the same time you should know that it was this horse, a few weeks later, who made a cheap postcard of my thigh when I went to cinch him up.

You could rope a little bit off this horse. He was better than I was, anyway. He wouldn't jump out from under a rope and you could heel calves off him. But you couldn't go to contests on him. He didn't like blasting out of the box with his ears pinned. He would jog up to a bunch of calves and let you snake them to the ground crew. He was kind of a working-man's horse. You could turn him out for the winter and wrangle him in the spring and he'd be solid. I haven't had a vet bill on him yet. Last year I tied a huge red ribbon around him and gave him to my son for Christmas. He looked at Cayenne in the snow, stunned, and I tried not to let tears come. None of this meant anything to Cayenne.

The very little roping I did when young was what they called doctor roping and had to do with dabbing a loop on a cow's head to immobilize her long enough to provide medical aid. . . . Doctor roping is also done for calves with the scours, and these little brutes are "heeled"; their back feet are roped and they are skidded to the branding fire—in my experience, a blowtorch. Dehorned, branded, castrated, vaccinated, they are turned loose traumatized. Most people nowadays use a chute and turn the calf on a table to do those things to him. But a lot of ranches don't have a table and they need someone so in love with roping he will heel calves all day long until lather forms around the latigo and cinch dees and linear rope burns form up and down the back of his hand from dallying. . . . When I first roped, I didn't know anything about dallying. It was hard-and-fast, the rope tied to the saddle horn. That's how contest calf ropers rope. They have to: they jump down and flank or leg the little cow and tie three legs with the pigging string, then throw their hands in the air. I don't like to get down and run all over the place like that. I'm getting too brittle. I like to stay mounted. Single steer jerkers also rope hard-and-fast, but dally roping—*dar la vuelta*—is an ancient and beautiful craft still understood by a large number of people, handed down from the days of the old-time *vaqueros,* the Mexicans and Californios, who nobody much remembers but who, with their hair-trigger spade-bit horses and braided *riatas* were the absolute best hands in the long and crazy history of the American West. The horses and vaqueros are dead and gone; but something remains: hackamore reinsmen and dally ropers.

When I first started to rope that way, the lunacy of roping 600-pound Corriente steers—Mexican horned cattle—without tying the end of the rope to the horn was obviated by the fact that I had misconducted my life to the point that it was, shall we say, in smithereens, and the prospect of losing a couple of fingers because I couldn't get my wraps didn't seem as catastrophic as it would when I was happy and had my accustomed, highly excitable fear of pain. This is the background of stoicism everywhere.

Times got better, but as luck would have it, there came a day when I couldn't find the saddle horn and broke my thumb in a few places, tearing the end off it. When I went to the emergency room, the nurse said, "Miss your dally?" and I said, "Just tell the doctor I hate pain." Nevertheless, he pulled my thumbnail out with a pair of needle-nosed pliers and told me I was going to lose it anyway. But I had started to learn to dally, with that crazily loose-ended lariat, relying on wrapping the rope around the saddle horn to stop heavy running cattle. . . .

When you first catch a steer you halfway wish you were through with it; the steer is hauling ass and that hard nylon rope heats to seeming incandescence when you run about 18 inches of it through your hand. At the same time, you have to run it a little; the steer is moving away and you need to let it slip as you start down to dally. Fundamentally, you should know how to run the whole rope and let it go, if you have to, without getting a turn around your hand. It's easy to lose a finger roping and almost as easy to lose a hand as a finger. ❧

THREE ON THE TRAIL

Here's another lesson in horse lore from Thomas McGuane, this one the record of a long chilly trek to a frozen campsite high above the Yellowstone Valley. McGuane shares some of the challenges and the literal pitfalls of sharing a horse with a friend on a snowy mountain climb. —G. E.

Excerpts from *An Outside Chance* by

THOMAS MCGUANE

Gene was sure there were enough horses. When I called him I said my friend Scott wanted to come and we would need another horse. I told him I had the saddles: a Mexican roping saddle; and an A-type, marked *Montana Territory,* in case we met any antiquarians in the mountains.

I drove south in the Yellowstone Valley the next morning; Scott got the gate and we headed up the road to the ranch that Gene stays on. It was a cold, late November day; Gene and Keith were putting the horses in the stock truck to take them up to the trailhead in Tom Miner Basin. . . .

Keith was dressed in his National Park Service coveralls and it was he who discovered we were shy a horse. Scott and I were hikers, though not so committed that we'd forgo the one horse. So I said we'd take that and they could pack our gear in the panniers and we'd meet them in camp.

Keith had secreted his little camp up some six-inch creek in the Gallatin Range; so we all hunkered around a clean piece of bare mud and scratched out directions. I made sure Scott and I had matches. We were going through an area of some grizzly concentration. I don't know what you bring for that, unless it is Librium and a glass of water.

We put the territorial saddle on a bunchy short mare that jumped every time you took off your coat, though Gene said she was "a good little bitch". . . Keith and Jim (another fellow from Bozeman) headed off in the pickup carrying the pack saddles, panniers, and all the gear. Scott and

49

I went with Gene in the stock truck. . . . We crossed the Yellowstone and headed up Tom Miner Basin, struggling for traction on the long, snowy canyon road. We parked the trucks at the top. Somebody had a tent there; and there was a small corral with four bales of hay in the snow.

Jim said, "Can you throw a diamond hitch?"

I said I could.

Scott and I led the four saddle horses and the two packhorses up to the corral and tied them. There was a lot of snow and we were going up another three or four thousand feet, Scott and I trading off on the antiquarian saddle, being too big to double-team the twitchy mare. . . .

Gene went ahead to cut a trail. Jim and Keith agreed to pack up and follow when they were done; and meanwhile Scott and I would start, trading off on the mare.

We started up the easy grade along Tom Miner Creek, Scott getting the first ride, up through the bare aspens and gradual snow-covered slopes dotted by dark knots of sage. . . . Then the canyon steepened during my turn on the horse, as I saw Scott fade, trudging behind in six inches of snow. The trail contoured around high on the north side, really quite steep. . . .

When Scott caught up, he confessed to thinking about grizzlies. "If one came after me," he said, "I would dodge around in those aspens, in and out, in and out, until somebody came and rescued me."

I trudged along behind as he gradually disappeared ahead. I noticed the snow getting heavy; and now the sky was deeply overcast and snow was beginning to pour down the canyon in a long sweep. After a while, I could see it streaming into the horse tracks, obscuring them. I transferred the matches to an inside pocket and mentally reviewed Jack London. I thought, When I get back, I'm going to buy a whole mess of horses so we never run out. . . .

I caught up with Scott in about half an hour. I climbed on the horse, not describing to him what he was in for as to wallowing. I noticed, though, that my boots disappeared into the snow, stirrups and all, making wakes. Scott remarked the horse looked like a cocktail waitress. So it was beginning to get to him, too.

In two trade-offs, we made it to the top. We looked back into the immense valley of the Yellowstone and rode (or walked) through the trees on a kind of plateau, Buffalo Horn Pass, where the Indian hunting parties crossed; and then to the Western slope and a tremendous view of the Gallatin drainage with white, jagged ranges angling in from the north.

The snow let up and we were in deep powder. When it was my turn to ride, I started down a long switchback that ended in the trees. Scott, on foot, decided to run straight down. At about the point I reached the trees, Scott was pinwheeling in a cloud of snow. Then the horse fell; though fearing getting hung up in the stirrups, I ejected U-2 style, before she hit the ground. The snow was so deep and soft that Scott and I and the horse wallowed around and made no very great attempt to get to our feet again. . . .

The horse was getting silly. When one of us rode ahead and the other reappeared, she jumped back in horror as though from a representative of a dog-food concern. And on the steep switchbacks, she slid down the snow on her haunches. I felt she was stunting and might pull anything next, an Immelmann turn, for example.

Then Scott galloped off through the trees, the trail making a soft white corridor and the speed of his departure producing a sun-shot curtain of snow. . . . Suddenly we were in camp: a wall tent half buried in powder and a pole corral. . . .

Keith and Jim arrived almost immediately with the pack stock. Keith complained that Gene had cut the trail too close to the trees, so that the pack animals banged the panniers all the way up; then, to Scott and me, he allowed as how the snow had been unexpectedly deep. . . .

Jim said, "The sorrel packhorse fell and slid 40 feet on its stomach and got up straight without spilling anything."

We all admired that. . . .

The sun was starting to go down at that. We had one more tent to put up. It took an hour to shovel the snow out of the site and get the ridgepole in place. The pile of split wood, fresh and lemony-smelling, was building in front of the first tent. And by about sundown the second tent was up, the heater in place. We threw in two shovelfuls of dirt so the bottom wouldn't burn out; put the sheet-metal tubes together to form the chimney and ran it up through the asbestos hole in the roof. We built a fire in it; and the snow inside started to melt in the warmth and form the mud hell that was necessary until the tent had aged a few days.

We went to the other tent about sundown. It was very cold; and we started to work on making dinner, spacing the job out with bourbon and one of those ersatz wines that is advertised right in there at half-time with Gillette razors and the Dodge Rebellion. Some of us were swaggering around with cigars.

Scott and I peeled potatoes and onions. Keith and Gene cooked some elk, sliced up a head of lettuce with a hunting knife. . . . We ate, greedily, for the first time that day. The mud was starting to deepen in the tent.

Somebody hauled some feed to the horses; I looked out the tent flaps and saw them picking precisely through the snow with their front hoofs for the pellets. . . .

Jim took the bucket of heated water off the sheepherder stove and started washing the dishes. . . .

"Where's Keith?" I asked. No one knew. After a while, I went to look for him. He was asleep in the other tent, laid out in the mud in his sleeping bag next to a pile of saddles. I put a couple of pieces of wood into the heater and the base of the chimney glowed cherry. When I walked back to the other tent, I stopped in the cold, still air and looked up at the stars. They seemed to swarm a matter of inches over my head. . . . I heard a coyote. I thought, I am on top of the earth and I don't work for the government.

Jim, Gene, and Keith all slept in the same tent because they were going to get up before dawn to look for elk. Scott and I rolled out our bags on the floor and turned off the Coleman lantern. For about half an hour, we could hear the banked-down stove crackle and see the rectangle of bright light around its door.

When the stove went out, the mud froze. I wished I had flattened out some of the mud under my bag because it froze in shapes not reciprocal to my body. I pulled the drawstring up tight around my face. I was warm in the good Ibex bag; but my head felt as if it was in a refrigerator. I put on my wool cap, feeling for it among my frozen, board-stiff socks and the hiking boots that were as rigid as building blocks.

I could hear when I woke up the next morning the other three crunching around outside, wrangling the horses and falling silent as they drank coffee in the tent. It was insultingly cold. . . .

We got up shortly and had a crackling fire going in the sheepherder stove. We made a pot of coffee and lazily divided a vast sheet of Missus So-and-So's breakfast rolls. I thawed my socks and boots in front of the stove; rivers of stream poured from them into the stove's open door.

When I stepped outside, I could see where the snow was trampled from the morning's wrangling. Their trail led across the small open meadow and over the rim, a soft trough in the perfect basin of snow. The light was tremendous and the sky formed an impressive light-shot blue dome, defined on the side of our camp by a row of snow-laden pines; and opposite us the glittering range of the Gallatins. A big lone spruce stood between us and the newly risen sun; full of snow and ice crystals, it exploded with the improbable brilliance of an Annunciation. There weren't words for it.

We put the bags in stuff sacks, straightened out the tent, and let the fire die. I printed a note and left it on a pannier, weighted with a jackknife.

Boys,

We're going to work our way on back. We'll leave the horse in the corral at Tom Miner Basin.   Tom and Scott

We got the bridle and saddle and headed out for the mare. A pine bough had shed its load of snow and her back was white and powdered with it as she stood in the glittering mountain light. I swept her dry while Scott warmed the bit in his hands.

We saddled the mare and took the long way home. ❧

WHISKEY RUN

Frank Harris records a truly wild west in his 1930 memoir My Reminiscences as a Cowboy. *It was a world of* caballeros, *of buffalo herds, and of duels at dawn. Harris's wry good humor captures the spirit and dangers of the work and sport and brawls of New Mexico at the turn of the century. —G. E.*

From *My Reminiscences as a Cowboy* by

FRANK HARRIS

O f course, little by little I got to know every one on the ranch and got to know, too, a good deal of the life that lay before me.

It was in March, I think, the buffalo grass just sprouting, when we resolved to start for the Rio Grande. Reece was to be our boss, Ford not going down, and the men all got $40 a month and a commission on the profits if we succeeded in bringing cattle up to Chicago.

The first days on the trail were not especially exciting. Every one was up about four o'clock, well before daybreak. The first man to awake would throw some buffalo chips (dry dung) on the fire; Peggy, the Indian cook, would soon swing a kettle on it and make the coffee, while some of us went down to the creek and washed our hands and faces, or even had a bath. Then we came fresh and eager to the hot coffee and hot biscuits, with a grill of buffalo steaks and fat bacon.

The air, even in early Spring and before sunrise, was warm, like fresh milk. Suddenly the curtain of the night would be drawn back, opal tints would climb up the eastern heaven, and these would change to mother-of-pearl, and break into streams of rose and crimson; in a moment the sun would show above the horizon, and at once it was day. After breakfast we would wash up and put things away in one of the wagons; Bent and the negroes would generally climb into a wagon and go to sleep again: the wagons would then be harnessed and commence their journey southward, while the rest of us would mount our bronchos and go on in front, detaching two of our number to drive the rest of the horses. In one respect these bronchos were something like Texan cattle—they all followed a leader and were therefore very easy to drive; bar anything unusual, one had simply to ride behind them, and an occasional flick of the whip or even a shout would keep them moving.

Five or six of us used to be perpetually riding together on young, fresh horses, summer day after summer day. Of course, there was all manner of skylarking and playing about. Some one would have mounted a new horse and want to prove it; immediately a bet would be made, and we would have a race to decide whether the new beast could gallop or not. If he turned out very fast, I would generally be sent off to get Shiloh or Blue Dick out of the herd and see how he would shape beside the fastest we had got. Shiloh was a thoroughbred horse, bought by Reece in Kentucky; as a three-year-old he had done a half-mile in forty-nine seconds, and over a mile was almost as fast as a Derby winner—was certainly as fast as good plating form. He could beat Blue Dick in a sprint or a scurry, but stretch the course from two miles to ten and Blue Dick would beat him a long way. I used to think that if you cantered Blue Dick for half a mile or so before you made her gallop, you could gallop until you were tired without tiring her.

I remember one occasion when I had to test her: we had camped about sixteen miles from Albuquerque, New Mexico. The men had been skylarking about with a prairie rattlesnake, trying to lift it on little twigs of sagebrush and throw it at each other. The prairie rattlesnake is very small, three feet or so in length, and thin as a whip-lash, whereas the forest rattlesnake is five or six feet long and thick as a girl's arm; but the prairie rattlesnake, though small, is just as venomous and ten times as quick and bad-tempered as his larger brother. The play ended, therefore, as might have been expected: the rattlesnake stung one of the men. . . .

As one of the lightest of the party, I was immediately called and told by Reece, our chief, to round up Blue Dick and ride into Albuquerque and bring out a bottle of whiskey, for it appeared that our small barrel had been allowed to get quite empty, and the poisoned man could only have a glass or so. I put a racing pad on Blue Dick's back and started with the boss's last words in my ears, "Don't spare the horse; Indian Pete is in a bad way." Pete was a silent, sulky creature, but the need was imminent, and though I was filled with anxiety about the mare I was to ride, I intended to do my best. I trotted the two hundred or three hundred yards to the creek and took her through the ford quite quietly. On the opposite bank I let her begin to canter, and I cantered for the next mile or so, till she had got quite dry and warm, and then I began to answer her craving for speed and let her go faster in a sort of hand-gallop. I kept at this for about half an hour and then loosed her out: in an incredibly short time I found myself on the outskirts of the town. I drew Blue Dick together for the last mile and let her go as hard as she could lay legs to ground. I pulled up at the first saloon in the main street, threw myself from her back, hitched her to a post, rushed in and got a bottle of whiskey, stuffed it in my pocket, and buckling my belt round it so as to keep it safe, rushed out, threw myself on Blue Dick's back, and was again racing down the street within two minutes, I should think, from the time I drew rein. Now, I said to myself, I must find out what Blue Dick can do. The heat was tremendous; it must have been quite ninety in the shade, perhaps a hundred and thirty-five in the sun; but the air was light, and though the mare was in a reek of sweat, she was breathing as easily as when she started. Gradually the fear of being late grew upon me, and I let her race as she would: the mare herself seemed to realize that speed was needed, for she settled down to her long stretching gallop, which I always compared to the gallop of a wolf, so tireless it seemed, and long and easy. Mile after mile swept past, and at last I saw the rise in the prairie which was the edge of the creek, and the few, mingy cottonwood trees that showed me I was almost home. Again and again I strained forward to look at the mare; there seemed no sign of distress in her; and then a sort of exultation in her tireless strength came to me, and wild joy that she was uninjured, and I shook her together with a shout, lifting her in her stride at the same time. At once she got hold of the bit, and before I could do anything had bolted with me at lightening speed. Down to the creek over the steep bank with a plunge into the water; across, up the opposite bank, and away like a mad thing. I had overshot the wagons by a hundred yards before I could pull her up. There were a dozen hands to take the whiskey bottle, which was fortunately whole. I threw myself off the mare and gave her to the care of Mexican Bob, to walk about; but almost at once any anxiety I had about Blue Dick vanished, for she set herself to munch some buffalo grass, and I saw that the long, hard gallop had done her no harm.

Strange to say, the whiskey didn't cure the Indian; he could not keep it on his stomach. He didn't even seem to try: from the first he believed that he was done for . . . he wrapped himself in his blanket and wanted to be left alone. When I saw him he was in a comatose state, and it was impossible to rouse him. We poured some whiskey down his throat, but it was thrown up again immediately: a couple of hours later he was dead.

That same night we buried him under one of the dwarf cottonwood trees near the bank of the creek, and there he probably sleeps quietly till this day. ❧

THE BIG BEEF FIELD

William Kittredge, who grew up on his father's huge desert ranch in the empty corner of southeastern Oregon, had a beginning that was very different from many of the writers in this collection. He was frightened of horses and bored with the cowboy's life, finding nothing glamorous in it, only knots of pain and fear. "I was frightened into mindlessness, and there was nothing I could do but pretend I wasn't. I had discovered a terrible vulnerability in myself which I think of not as cowardliness but as an ability to imagine too much." —G. E.

Excerpts from *Hole in the Sky* by

WILLIAM KITTREDGE

By the time I was eight, my grandfather had determined that my cousin Jack and I were plenty old enough to drive cows and begin our education in working-man horseback traditions and the demands of manhood.

On a day I recall as ecstatic, he bought my older cousin and me a couple of new saddles from the leather-smelling saddlemaker's shop in Lakeview. Mine was engraved and cost one hundred and twenty-five dollars; for many years it was the most expensive thing I owned, and I loved it as the surest part of what I was going to become. It was confirmed that I was going to be a horseman. All I had to do was stay tough enough.

The first real day of work set standards in rigor, at least in my mind, which were never really broken. In the early-morning darkness of a rainy day in April our cowhand crew headed out to gather dry cows (cows without calves, they were not giving milk) from the swamps of what was called the Big Beef Field. And big it was, five miles square and half flooded by spring runoff, the sloughs deep enough to swim a horse.

Though my mother worried, my grandfather said something to the effect that nothing out there in the Big Beef Field was going to hurt that goddamned kid, which was supposed to make me proud. I was piss-your-pants scared. In that country of desert and small creeks we never learned to swim; it was one of our disabilities. But no need to worry, my grandfather said. Your horse can swim, just stick with your horse. And it was true.

Out there in the Big Beef Field my old horse named Moon was swimming half the time. The hides of those heavy-bellied cows ran slick with mud. Moon would pause as he labored through the sucking black mud in the tulebeds, I would grab the saddle horn with both hands, and he would go lunging out into the deep water which geysered up on all sides. I was frightened deep into mindlessness, and there was nothing to do but pretend I wasn't. I had discovered a terrible vulnerability in myself which I think of not as cowardliness but as an ability to imagine too much.

It is still there. I can't swim, and I am terrified of absolute heights, where a fall (or, more to the point, a leap) would be without recourse. This, of course, was an unfortunate fallibility in a boy with plans to become a horseback hero. And that first day wasn't really such a difficult day by buckaroo standards. By midafternoon we were turning our three thousand or so dry cows through the outside fence on the east side of Warner. My grandfather thought we ought to trail them along the beginnings of their fifty-mile walk to the deserts where they would summer. A couple of hours, he said.

But someone said something like "those kids got to be sent to the house, they're done in." My grandfather inspected us, saw it was true, and shook his head as if appalled by our sorry, worn-out childishness. Maybe it was there, at that moment, that I began learning my lesson. We were sent to the house, about ten miles, soaking wet and deeply chilled, and that terrifying day vanishes into a memory of riding on and on along a muddy levee bank into the deepening gloom of overcast twilight. And I made it. I was not absolutely doomed. I could make it.

That summer Jack and I started spending time on the desert, "out with the buckaroos." It was a couple of months on horseback, without any momma. It was our true beginning. How glorious it sounded. And it was, in many ways.

The first day lasted forever. It was our task to ride drag behind a couple of hundred meandering Hereford bulls as they were moved out of Warner toward the deserts to the east. Slowly, so slowly, we followed those loitering thick-skinned creatures up Greaser Canyon, their asses green with shit as they switched at flies, to a place called Hill Camp, where the four-horse chuck wagon was set up for the night. Before it was done I was almost sick with boredom. But I ought to have been sicker; I should have foreseen the future, and recognized a lifetime trailing livestock as a fate to be avoided at most any cost. It was twilight when we turned our horses loose to roll in the dust and run with the other seventy-some head in the remuda.

The cook, a woman named Lois Clair, clanged the dinner bell. The men laughed and joked in their impervious way. They were not used to the idea of a woman in camp. Kenny Clair, her young husband, the camp tender, usually known as the wrango boy, eyed them nervously. So did we, the owner's kids. We were facing our new lives, a couple of goddamned kids in a cow camp.

It is impossible to know what those men thought, and most of them are dead now. But they treated us with rough decency, and saw us through. Those men were good to us, good enough. So was Lois Clair, a flint-hearted girl as I recall, but she would not let anybody pick on us, even though she made it clear she thought we'd been spoiled with too much mothering as it was. We ate our first meal in silence and then ran to climb the little cliffs behind the spring, where we found an old deteriorating box of dynamite nobody knew was there.

Within a couple of weeks I was refusing to wash. My lips and cheeks had sunburned, and I was accustomed to misery, sort of happy inside it, dirty and stubborn, gone somewhat feral. My schoolboy cheeks had cracked into deep scabbed-over furrows that bled and healed and broke open to heal again. Trying to remember those days I think I understand how children go naturally wild. It's like retreating into a cave, and finding the world is only a distant, unimportant noise. But maybe that's only the story I'm telling myself. I wonder if I know anything true about that child who wouldn't bathe, or even wash his crusted face, who stank. The men sent me down to the little creek below Sage Hen Springs with a bar of soap. Clean up, they said, holding up heavy scrub brushes, or we'll do it for you. I hated them.

The next summer, the straps on my new cowboy boots rubbed sores into the calves of my legs. The dim scars are there yet. Every day was a new day with my pain, saddle up, and nothing was real but pain; it was my life, everything else was unreal. It must never have occurred to me that I might ask someone for help, or simply take a pocketknife to the damned bootstraps. I don't think it was a misery I loved.

But it gave me excuses for fucking off. Along with stoic self-reliance I was learning the commonsense skills called "soldiering," those of insulating and protecting myself, lying back. Let some other damned fool do the volunteering. It was a lesson in goldbricking, and a sad lesson for a boy, which is taking a long time to unlearn.

"If I can stand this," I thought, "I can stand all they got, all my life." Children think such things. I lived with a secret pride, even in my shame; I loved myself, and knew I would never have to kill myself, ever, because I could stand the pain. I wonder if it's an understanding that will sustain me through the crippling miseries of old age. ❧

FROM POINT TO DRAG

Dayton Hyde is a cowboy's cowboy and a thoroughgoing naturalist at the same time. He is the founder and manager of The Black Hills Wild Horse Sanctuary in South Dakota. His family continues to operate their second-generation cattle ranch in the Upper Williamson Valley of south-central Oregon. He runs his ranch holistically while never losing sight of the intricacies of "cowboy etiquette." In a sliver from his delightful memoir of ranching life, Wilderness Ranch, *Hyde celebrates the cowboy life in which it was not necessary to talk—one simply knew where to be and when, and never stirred up the herd. —G. E.*

Excerpts from *Wilderness Ranch* by

DAYTON O. HYDE

In those days, we moved the Yamsi cattle out in the fall to the winter hay supply, instead of keeping them at the ranch as we do now. In November it meant a four-day drive from Yamsi to the old Blooming camp ranch, the BK, on the north side of the Bly valley, and in the spring another four-day drive back to the headwaters of the Williamson, when the range was ready for turning out cattle. The fall drive was easy since the calves had all been weaned from the cows. Spring was a different matter, for we left the BK with about five hundred cows and nearly as many tiny freshly branded calves. In a May dawn, we eased them out of a holding field into the long lane formed by split-rail fences, weathered and moss encrusted, on each side of the road. Those fences were a curse, since in their tumbled condition they often let a cow cross but kept a horse from following her. From the field we left a muddy track westward, past the Fitzpatrick place, the Labores Ranch, and down the sagebrushed hill to where the spring-swollen North Fork of the Sprague River crowded itself dangerously under a flimsy bridge.

If the river was down there would be fishermen on the bridge, and the cattle would be afraid to cross. If the river was high, the torrent often swirled over the bridge as well as under, and calf after calf was crowded over the hidden edges and swept away. Some drowned; some surfaced fifty feet downstream, and were cast with the driftwood on some willowed island or another, from which it took a long rope, repeatedly tossed, to capture them and drag them ashore. I shudder to remember.

We held the herd in the lane just beyond the river to let the calves catch up and dry off from their ordeal, as well as to let the men ride for survivors down the stream. We had to guard the bridge, for often the calves would break back, bound for the point where they last sucked, and hit the angry torrent as though it were a shallow mud puddle. When you guarded the drag of a herd of cows and small calves, let but one calf turn from the herd to face you and you were in trouble, for then the rest would follow suit and run back. Once they had broken past you, you seldom had horsemen enough to turn them, but were forced to let them run, losing the hard-won miles until you could control them again.

As we left the lane, the cows, following the road, turned northward, then westward, up over the rolling hills. Sagebrush gave way to timber as they climbed. They seemed to sense now that they were headed for the Yamsi range, for out of the dragging resisting herd came leaders, sucking the rest with them up the hillsides and switchbacks, cracking the herd behind them like a whip as they trotted down hills while the drag was laboring up. Two men rode the point, two along the flanks, and the rest pounded the drag. The timber grew thicker now with islands of impenetrable young bullpine and scratchy tangles of mountain mahogany, as we dragged along the sleeping horse form of Charlie Mountain.

The men in the drag fought a constant war to keep the tired calves traveling along, trying to keep them from lying down unnoticed in the brush while the herd passed on. Now and then a cow would drop back to the bulging rear of the herd, thick with calves, find her calf among the bawling masses, and go on ahead with him. It was easier by far for her to lead her calf than it was for us to push him.

Noon usually found us on the Blue Creek flats, near the site of the old abandoned Indian lumber mill. There was water here for the cows, and an open meadow on which we could rest the herd and not risk the calves breaking back unseen through some handy thicket. We let the calves suck so that if they broke back in the future bound for where they had sucked last, they would return here instead of heading ten miles back to the BK.

Ern Morgan and I rode point, him on one side and me on the other, steering the leaders between us up the road. If the leaders slowed down, going up a hill, it was understood between us that we'd take a bunch and push them up the incline. Going downhill we'd brake the leaders by riding ahead of them, Morgan and I, side by side, blocking the road, letting them travel or eat up just as much ground as we saw fit. Even on the flat, the point men set the pace for the whole herd, and all the men in the drag had to do was try to keep pace with the leaders.

Ern was the best point man I ever saw. He had an uncanny ability to outguess a cow. Without ever getting his horse out of a walk, he would watch ahead and pick out a place where a lead cow would naturally stray, taking the bunch with her.

Morgan was always there ahead of time, sitting quietly on his horse, a Bull Durham cigarette clamped stolidly and unlit in his set lips. Only the faint trace of a smile as a cow would turn as predicted from the road, look longingly in his direction, and then, since he blocked the way, turn and go obediently off down the road. Every quiet triumph of his meant saving the rest of us ten or fifteen minutes getting the herd pointed back down the road. At the end of the day fifteen minutes might be the difference between winning or losing, getting there or being trapped by darkness on the road.

Morgan and I seldom spoke; we shared a professional pride in being able to work together without speaking. For him to have advised me of a potential disaster up ahead would have been a slight to brood about for the rest of the day. To have let one see the other at a trot would have been to admit that he had been outwitted by a cow.

A good cowboy nursed his horse carefully, for on such a cattle drive he had to make one mount last the distance, and there was no predicting what disaster might befall tomorrow, when having fresh horseflesh left under one's saddle might save the day. A cowboy lost caste by galloping a horse after a cow; he turned her back at a trot if he could—but the best cowboy would have been quietly in position and prevented the cow from getting away in the first place. The buckeroo who learned his trade by watching the unreality of movie cowboys at a constant gallop was quickly fired from one outfit after another until he learned to settle down and handle the animals in the quietest possible manner.

There were times, of course, when the men could pound, pound, pound on the tail end of a herd, and all the shouting and cursing in the world wouldn't move them. But there were times when men spoke in a whisper or not at all, and the animals watched for the slightest excuse to spook. Wise to the sounds of the trail, the cattle were moved or soothed by only a slight difference in tone in the shouts they heard. I can close my eyes now and see out of the darkness that is the past the long herd trailing through the fragrant, sun-drenched sage, see the dust billowing in beige clouds over the drag, hear the cows bawling endlessly for their calves, and the men in the drag shouting and cursing. "Yippeeaoh! Git up there you——!" And over it all, Morgan's call drifting back over the herd from his position at the point, chastising cowboy and critter alike, whoever felt guilty. "Give 'er 'elllll!"

Cattle travel best if not driven at all, and the challenge was to keep the whole herd nodding peacefully, nose to tail down the road, eating up the miles at their own pace, each cow with room to avoid eating up the others' dust, with her calf anchored firmly behind, and with no appreciable bulge of stragglers in the rear of the herd.

The sight of five hundred fine, big, uniform Bar Y cows spread over a couple of miles of forest road was something to watch. People traveled for miles to see them, often arriving at the most inopportune moments, in time to either spook the cows off the road or catch a cowboy with his pants down in the sage. Gordon Barrie would be there to count the cows for the bank; there were mortgages in those days too. There were visitors who drove out to appreciate quality, and those, wiser than we, who sensed that what they were seeing was the last gasp of an era of Western history, a scene soon to be lost, swept away by the tides of change.

Often some rubbernecking stranger would roll down his window and ask me as I rode the point, "How many cattle you got in this herd, son?" Instead of the five hundred we actually had, I'd tip my hat back, scratch my dusty head with a buckskinned glove, chew a moment on a sagebrush twig, and venture, "Hell, I don't know, Mister. Coupla thousand, at least."

And the man would say, "Well I'll be damned. Why, I was just telling the wife here there must be a couple of thousand head!" He'd go back to town a whole lot happier having seen two thousand cattle than he'd have been with just the actual five hundred.

By nightfall that first day we'd crossed the Sycan River just north of Beatty, and bedded them down in a holding field west of the bridge at Bart Shelley's place. We camped outside by choice, for Bart had only two rooms and one of these was filled to the ceiling with old magazines. He chewed tobacco, too, and wasn't overly careful about where he spat, generally fouling the shoes of the fellow he was talking to through the corral fence. When you went to sit down in a chair in his house you looked where you were sitting then plunked down fast, for he could hit the seat with a dollop faster than you could with your rear.

Bart owned a big black bucking horse named Blackhawk, which might have gone on to be another Five Minutes Till Midnight had not Bart been too proud of him to sell him to the rodeo strings. Blackhawk was well into his twenties, an advanced age, when he finally went into the professional rodeo circuit and was a great horse even then, being chosen as a finals horse in the Pendleton Roundup. But his career, late in starting, was short lived, for a cattle truck overturned with him and he had to be destroyed. I still remember Bart shuffling up to the campfire, a few scraggly gray hairs cropping from beneath his battered old hat, "By Gawd, boys," he'd say. "I got a black horse over in that corral I wish one of you Bar Y cowboys would ride. Why, he's plumb gentle." But the cowboys knew the horse and no one ever tried.

By the time the calves had been mothered up and quit trying to head back toward Bly, the chuck wagon had generally caught up to the herd. A cowboy or two slipped off toward the lights of Beatty to the south for a little tipi crawling, but most of us were too tired to do more than lie around the campfire, listening to the sounds of cattle cropping the grass, the snuffle of contented horses, noses buried deep in their burlap nose bags, and the sizzle of steaks frying atop the iron stove. The sagebrush was full of ticks, and lumpy under our bedrolls; crushed by our bodies, its perfume was too heady to be pleasant, but we slept the sleep of the dead, too tired to care.

Dawn came early and nippy with Morgan coughing up a storm with his Bull Durham hack. Other than to swear at the cold, no one talked. One by one we crunched down to the banks of the Sycan to douse our faces in the cold river water, and from that instant we were wide awake. Still nobody talked much as we huddled about, watching the cook fry eggs on a stove that had no bottom, with drafts shoveled in the dirt along the sides. The idea was to creep as close to the stove as you dared without getting in the cook's way and arousing his ire. He had a way of accidentally spilling hot water on one's pant leg. Coffee black as night, so black your spoon disappeared from sight a half inch down into the murk. Only when I left home and his coffee did I find out what had been ailing me.

From the Sycan bridge, the road bent north again, on past Tim Brown Springs, a willowy, quaking, treacherous boggy mess, lined with the bones of thirsty cattle that had waded in but never waded out. We ganged up on the spring side of the herd to keep the cattle heading down the road.

From there the road slanted up the hillside and climbed over the jagged rimrocks to the broad flat top of the table-land. It was a rough place to meet a car, and we generally did. Once it was a drunk Indian in a big black Chrysler, who came down the hill leaning on his horn, scattering cattle over the edge, and once they headed down there was no stopping them. He offered us all a drink and took it as right unfriendly that we wouldn't stop and be sociable. We were two days gathering the cows and the calves.

The tableland was a vast lava plateau, whose rocky reaches were broken only occasionally by oases of sand, covered with the brown straw deposit from the thick growth of Ponderosa pines that flourished in islands there. Now and then one of these islands would boast a stream of cool, milky spring water, its shores lined with groves of tremble-leaved aspens, a water source which flowed off the barren lands and left in its wake a green grassy draw or swale.

At Eldon Springs there was a log corral for our horses, water, a lovely grove of aspen, and a lush meadow on which the cattle could feed and bed down for the night. Most of the cattle stayed, but some were eager now for home, and during the evening went on ahead with their calves. We looked the other way, for it would be that many less to drive come daybreak, and they would leave a set of tracks in the road for the others to follow. In the morning a band of antelope raced smoothly across the horizon, mule deer bounded for a cleft in the rim, a flock of great sage grouse almost as big as turkeys roared in off the flats for water. We had come thirty miles from the BK and still had another six to go to the edge of the Bar Y range, at Teddy Powers' meadow.

Sometimes in the clear visibility of the early morning, before the rising heat from the rocks made the air shimmer with mirages, we saw a flash of wild horses daring the open expanse between one forest island and another, moving back into the safety of the thickets for the day. Pintos, sorrels, bays, blacks, buckskins, motley browns. For a few years there was an isolated herd of blues, the color of blue velvet. I watched them often through binoculars. You could see the old grandmother, ancient, wide-sprung in gaunt ribs, and spavined. There was an assortment of daughters of every age, and a young barrel-chested stallion, all related, all blue, broken-hooved, black manes tangled like the hair of a madwoman. But they would run like the wind over a shattering fester of broken lava rock here in this garden of the Devil; their hard, flinty hooves rang like bells on the tumbled rock ocean as they fled at the first glimpse of a rider's hat on the horizon. ❧

HIGH MEADOW SOLITUDE

Laura Bell came to Wyoming from Kentucky and Tennessee in 1977, fresh from college, to herd sheep. She worked on a very large ranch pieced together by Mormons at the turn of the century, and worked for the grandson of the original homesteader. To live and work alone out on the range is a hardship for anyone, and Laura learned, firsthand, the joys and difficulties of solitude, the ways it can corrode and embolden the human spirit.

To keep track of time on a job whose only framework is darkness and light, she made a calendar of days in watercolor, noting changes in weather and activities in her herd of 1,500 lambs and ewes, and the hardships endured: blizzards, thunderstorms, hundred-mile-an-hour winds.

In 1980 she moved to a cattle ranch in Shell, Wyoming, and cowboyed for five years, moving from there to a job in the Forest Service as a range conservator. She now lives and works near Salt Lake City. —G. E.

Excerpts from the personal journal of

LAURA BELL

April 10—*Coon Creek Camp*—Where did this wind come from? The sun is strong, but the wind is howling out of the northwest with some angry purpose. My sheepwagon rocks, trying to sprout wings.

The west is a streak of haze where the wind has whipped the dust up from the ground and into the sky. Willy, my horse, stands unprotected at the end of his picket line, head to the ground and butt to the wind. Louise, my dog, scratched at the door and is asleep now with her head on my thigh.

This country is empty and endless when the wind blows like this. I am lonesome today.

April 11—Coon Creek Camp—They brought my sheep out this afternoon. I didn't think I'd be so glad to see them come down off the trucks, but it changes the quality of living here. It gives me a reason for being out here and forces me out into this wild weather. The land begins to take shape when there are sheep on it, and my day is fleshed out by the movement and responsibility of caring for them.

This is our beginning. From here the lambs will feed and grow, and we will all be nomads following the melting snows and new grass up from this broken desert country to the high mountain pastures where we will spend the summer at 10,000 feet. For a season, we are family, this bleating wave of ewes and lambs, two dogs, one horse, and I.

April 12—Coon Creek Camp—A brilliant day. I was able to get a good look at my sheep today and begin to pick out the markers, the odd-colored ones that will stand out as signs that I have all my sheep in one place. Already I've lost one lamb, found dead this morning where the sheep had bedded last night in a tight knot. In the first days, the weak ones will die quickly.

April 16—"V" Camp—The sound of John's pickup woke my bones at 5 o'clock this morning, but by the time he arrived at camp I had pulled on my clothes and started the fire. We had coffee, then moved my camp to the west up into what is called the "V" because the land lies between two highways that merge into one, forming the ten mile letter. The morning was still and golden, and the sheep moved easily, loosening the smell of sage and flushing up small birds as we trailed. The ridge where my wagon is set is rough and high with grand views.

April 28—Wire Pond Camp—It's been raining for four days, and I'm still in this miserable hole of a camp. I have to ride so far just to get to where I can see my sheep, and I'm stuck out in the rain most of the day. I have mud in my hair and smell like a wet horse, but the first Indian paintbrushes are beginning to pop out in the rain and every crack, every hoofprint is filled with water and turning green.

May 7—Twin Ponds Camp—McCullough Peaks—Windy and cold today, but the sun finally made it through after four solid days of rain and Wyoming wind. My sheep have been feeding on the flats above the Twin Ponds.

Riding these last few days has been a chore. The winds have been pelting us with rain, sleet, and even a little hail. I've been so bundled up with my head down to the wind, I've hardly seen a thing around me.

May 16—Bench Camp—McCullough Peaks—I lost my horse today. I lost Willy to the wild horses, and there's no one to tell, no one to fix it or bring him back.

I woke this morning to strong gusty winds and the sight of three wild horse bands showing off for each other in the

low hills above my camp. It was Willy who woke me, stamping and snorting and hitting the end of his picket chain that was wound tightly through the sage, his eyes bolted to the horses. The stallions had bunched the mares into three tight knots that circled and swang, finally slowing into a still point with only the wind howling and the stallions themselves moving through the air along the inner edges of their mares.

From a quarter mile away, we could feel the tension. Willy was charged by it and wanted to be gone into the middle of it. The wind and the horses had riled him up into an animal I didn't recognize. He was not the horse that would hang his head through my sheepwagon door to snuffle at my coffee and take cookies from my hand or the one that would make mischief around the wagon, stretching his neck and bending almost to his knees to lip the edge of the dogfood pan until he worked it out from underneath the wagon to eat. I didn't see the horse whose ear would cock when I called his name from the wagon steps and crooned silly words of endearment to him. I had come to think of him as a human presence. A friend. A joker member of the family. But this morning, he was of some other ancient race, sweated and strained to the primitive energies on the hill and oblivious to oats, cookies, camp, or home. He was in some other place.

So, I was careful. I tied him up short to the wagon to saddle him, and instead of dropping the halter to the ground to bridle him, I slipped it down around his neck and fastened the buckle. Just to be safe.

I was careful. I bridled him and dropped the halter to the ground and led him a few steps away from camp, away from the horses to get on him, but as I led him away he reared and pulled back, ducking his head and pulling himself right out from the bridle. And there he stood, saddled, his head bare and high and frozen. I began to sweat, and willed him to stay. I drew back from him toward the oat can at the side of the wagon and began to rattle the lid softly, sifting the oats through my fingers. I crooned. I grovelled. You can have them all. Anything you want. But his head swang around high to the horses on the hill, and he knew he was loose. He moved away from us to the edge of camp with the stiff-legged staccato movements of exhilaration. And then he was gone, bucking, twisting, stirrups flying, and beating at his flanks. Gone into the hills. As he became smaller, the bands began to move in the distance, the stallions aware of his presence and confused by it, circling around their mares, the bands circling around each other, and all disappearing from my view in a roiling wave.

It's evening now. The sheep are well scattered, inching their way with noses to the ground towards the knob where they will bed tonight. My horse is gone. Tomorrow is my twenty-fifth birthday, and it's starting to rain.

May 22—Bench Camp—McCullough Peaks—John finally made it into camp early this morning, chained up on all fours to get through the mud and worried about what he might find. One of Smokey's herders that herds east of here towards the highway had found my saddle in a gully on his range—the cinch split apart. Then, yesterday, Willy had wandered into his camp, lonesome and cut up and looking for oats. Not being a mare, he'd had no place with the wild horses and had been fought out of the bands by the stallions. Through the sheepherder grapevine, John had heard the news late last night and was at my camp at dawn with another horse for me, a sweet sorrel mare with a delicate face, and a "two story" birthday cake, made a week ago by him and decorated with plastic flowers, but undelivered because of the rains.

The mare is new and has no name. She has the bright-eyed look of a tree in fall color, so I've named her "Maple," and welcome her into our camp while Willy heals.

Lady, Louise, and I are celebrating with big slices of chocolate cake, but Maple seems only to like the icing.

June 29—Little Mountain—We scrambled up out of the Slide Rock trail about noon today, hot, gritty, and grinning, to the high sage benches of Little Mountain where we will camp for several weeks at 7,000 feet. We have made it, and this is the prize for our long days on the trail.

We have climbed the face of the mountain this morning on a trail that picks its way up between cliffs and around tilting slabs of sliderock. It's a trail worthy of the curses I've bestowed upon it. Easy for sheep. Rigorous, but not dangerous for a hiker. But for a horse with slippery iron shoes, nearly impassable. We made it, but not without many false starts and backtracks to find the single spots of grace that would let us through.

We are tired, all of us. The grass around the wagon is sprinkled with spring beauties and shooting stars and is lush enough to make little beds around us where we are sprawled, dead to the world.

September 11—Half Ounce Creek—Bighorn Mountains—There have been a few times this summer when I wanted something more. Something exotic or fancy, maybe a touch of sophistication. Maybe it was just wanting a long hot shower and a night on the town, and when I thought that way, I thought it wouldn't be so hard to leave. That I would be glad to get back where life is softer. But, I think in some ways I have never been so pampered as I've been here, even though most people would say that this life is a bleak one. Today with the snow falling and the quakers across the river barely turning to gold, this feels like my place in the world. ❧